Praise for
If I Ignore It, It Will Go Away

"The Erma Bombeck of the Bible strikes again with another zany and often poignant look at everyday life. You'll laugh out loud as Marsha discusses topics ranging from dealing with in-laws to keeping pet guinea pigs alive."

—MICHAEL MORRIS, author of *A Place Called Wiregrass* and *Slow Way Home*

"With plenty of humor, honesty, and insight, Marsha encourages us to lift our heads out of the sand and see life for what it really is—both tremendously challenging and amazingly rewarding. So come up for some air and have a good read. It just might change your life."

—MARTHA BOLTON, author of numerous books of humor including *Didn't My Skin Used to Fit?*

Praise for
101 Simple Lessons for Life
by Marsha Marks

"*101 Simple Lessons for Life* is a wonderful mix of the serious and the lighthearted. This is a jewel of a book!"

—FRANCINE RIVERS, author of numerous books including *Redeeming Love*

"In *101 Simple Lessons for Life,* Marsha Marks shows us how to take faith seriously and life with a sense of humor. This is a poignant, insightful, and often hilarious book."

—LAURIE BETH JONES, author of *Jesus CEO* and *Teach Your Team to Fish*

"*101 Simple Lessons for Life* is filled to overflowing with humor and spiritual wisdom. Every page is like an intimate visit with a trusted friend who almost always makes you laugh."

—CLAIRE CLONINGER, songwriter, speaker, and author of *When the Glass Slipper Doesn't Fit* and the E-mail from God series

"I love to laugh unexpectedly, and that's what I did many times throughout this little volume. But what strikes me most about *101 Simple Lessons for Life* is that the truth in this book is old, and so is the wisdom, but because they come through one person's experience and words, they are fresh and alive and recognizable. We live this stuff every day but may be utterly unaware."

—TRACY GROOT, author of *The Brother's Keeper*

"*101 Simple Lessons for Life* is a pocketful of gems wrapped in paper binding! This is a book to be treasured."

—ANGELA HUNT, author of *The Shadow Women*

If I Ignore It,
It Will Go Away

If I Ignore It, It Will Go Away

AND OTHER LIES
I THOUGHT WERE TRUE

Marsha Marks

Author of 101 SIMPLE LESSONS FOR LIFE

WATERBROOK
PRESS

IF I IGNORE IT, IT WILL GO AWAY
PUBLISHED BY WATERBROOK PRESS
2375 Telstar Drive, Suite 160
Colorado Springs, Colorado 80920
A division of Random House, Inc.

Scriptures quoted or paraphrased are Matthew 5:37 (page 57), Hebrews 11:25 (page
58), Deuteronomy 32:35 (page 68), Luke 6:27-31 (page 76), Mark 15:34 (page 93),
Psalm 51:17 (page 96), Matthew 7:1 (page 122), Luke 18:1-8 (page 125), Matthew
9:11-13 (page 126), Ecclesiastes 3:11 (page 136), Matthew 6:25-34 (page 141),
Matthew 3:17 (page 150), and Isaiah 53:6 (page 154).

ISBN 1-57856-698-3

Published in association with Yates & Yates, LLP, Attorneys and Counselors, Orange,
California.

Printed in the United States of America

*This book is dedicated to anyone
who ever thought, as I once did:
The truth will go away—
if I just ignore it long enough.*

Contents

Lies I Believed About People and Relationships

Introduction

*A*s you read this book, you may come up with two questions. The answer to both of them is *yes*. Yes, the stories are true. And, yes, I really was that stupid.

Lies I Believed About Home

You can't burn
hard-boiled eggs.

❧

$\mathcal{I}$ was running around like a person with a naturally hyper disposition who has too many things to do and too little time to do them—rushing through the house like someone who knows her six-year-old will be home from school in less than an hour and that whatever is not done by then will be put off for another day. That's when I realized I was starving and put four eggs on to boil. I turned them on high, because who has the time to wait?

Then I went back into my office. Now, when I am working on a deadline, I am able to ignore all sounds. So when I heard the sound of the first explosion, I kept writing, because I was so focused. Then I heard a second explosion and looked up from my computer screen, wondering briefly if the explosions needed my attention. When two more explosions ripped though the front part of my home, I got up from my writing chair and went to investigate.

What I saw was not a pretty sight. It turns out that hard-boiled eggs, if left in a pan with no water on high heat for about forty-five minutes, become objects in motion, shattering as they explode. And when they hit the wall, they become embedded into the drywall, something I have called PEEP: Putrid Exploding Egg Pieces.

After four such explosions, we had PEEP everywhere—on the floor, the counter, the utensils, the cupboards, the refrigerator, and even outside the kitchen. Yes, across the hall from the kitchen, some PEEP had even hit the door of our guest bathroom.

It was such a mess—and I don't clean the house well under normal circumstances—that I just turned off the stove and walked out. I did think about calling the dog in, but I wasn't sure if egg and eggshell are okay for the dog. I mean, I'd only recently learned that chocolate could kill dogs. Who knew what PEEP could do? The smell alone was enough to knock a dog flat. Plus, I didn't think I could lift that dog high enough for her to lick all the PEEP off the walls and ceiling fan.

The egg explosion was especially frustrating because just the week before I had burned rice. Not many people burn rice. But if you put rice on the stove to boil, even at a low temperature, and then you leave the room for an hour, you will have a terrible smell and blackened rice, and I don't mean Cajun flavored. (But I can now tell you the difference between burned rice and burned eggs. Rice doesn't explode.)

My husband, Tom, is a man of few words. And a dry wit. When Tom came home after the burned rice incident, he looked at me and said five words: "Cooking is a participatory activity."

What he means, of course, is it takes involvement to be a good cook. Or at least not to ruin things you meant only to boil. And *that*, I suppose, is the basic failure of things I like to cook: I don't stay with them to the end. I leave them on high and run away. And you just can't take your mind off what you are making and expect it to turn out any good.

I can keep a house just like my mother-in-law does.

❦

y mother-in-law is Martha Stewart on steroids. By that I mean she can clean and set a table and raise three kids, all the while making homemade waffles with heated syrup for breakfast.

Once, while a neighbor was at my home and I was bemoaning how messy it was, the neighbor tried to comfort me. "Look," she said. "I'm sure Tom didn't grow up in a perfect home." Then she looked at Tom and said, "Now tell your wife your mother didn't always keep a spotless house, did she?"

Tom and I looked at each other and burst into laughter. Because the truth is, as Tom sheepishly admitted, "Well, yes, she actually did keep a pretty spotless house."

We have actual recorded history of the fact that Shirley's home was decorated and clean, and every day a three-course hot dinner was on the table within seconds of the time she had announced dinner would be served.

My husband says that he never remembers going to McDonald's as a kid, even though there was a new one in his town. (By contrast, our daughter can never remember *not* going to McDonald's. We refer to Ronald McDonald as "our chef, Ron.")

Now, Shirley would deny all this Martha Stewart stuff. She would wave her hand over her collection of Hummels and over her perfectly decorated home and over the eight desserts she puts out for Christmas and say, "This is just what is expected of a wife and a mom."

But I'm here to tell you the truth. If my husband expected that from me, it ain't what he got. I tried. When I first married Tom, I tried to be like the woman who raised him. For example, I watched her press her husband's work shirts, and I tried to press Tom's shirts—until I realized I was ruining them. I either burned the shirts or overstarched them or left them in the washer to mildew. (Yes, that actually happened.) Or I would knock a button off with the iron and put the shirt in a pile to be fixed later, until one day my husband went to reach for a shirt and they were *all* in a pile to be fixed later. I'm just not my mother-in-law.

And the whole heated syrup thing? I'd never even heard of heated syrup before I married Tom. But one morning when I was having a major domestic streak, I made pancakes—from scratch. (You take this box of stuff and add eggs and milk and then pour. It's not as easy as it sounds.) When I presented the whole beautiful stack of pancakes to my husband (after throwing away the four that were burned), he said, "The pancakes look great, but the syrup is cold."

"Yeah," I said. "It's been in the refrigerator."

"Well…" he said, "let's heat it. My mom used to always heat the syrup."

"Are you out of your mind?" I wanted to say. But instead I said, "That's a good idea."

Which it was. For that one day. But if he thought heated syrup was going to be an everyday occurrence in our home, he was nuts. Too many things to remember.

And holidays were really crazy. I realized after just one Christmas at my in-laws' home that the phrase Hillary Clinton made popular was true: It would take a village if I were going to repeat that dinner at my home. A village of caterers. And Shirley had done it by herself.

It was a sad day when I realized that by the standards I saw in my mother-in-law, I was a failure. So I had to talk with my husband and say, "What she is— is great. But it ain't me."

And he sat down and said, "I married you because I wanted you, not someone else." Tom said I was making us both miserable by trying to be someone I wasn't. He wanted me to develop the gifts I'd been given; we would cope with the things I was not.

So today when we entertain at our home, I let someone else clean and someone else cook. I'm the person who chats up the crowd. That's what I do well. And if no one is there to clean or cook, we entertain in a messy home and eat takeout.

In my old age, as I'm learning more truth every day, I'm learning that what I have is enough and, if I don't have what someone else has, that's okay.

If you visit my mother-in-law, you will get a clean home and a nice meal, on matching dishes. If you visit me and you're allergic to dust, you might want to bring an antihistamine. And if there are leftovers in the refrigerator, I promise to check for mold before I serve them.

But, whether you visit Shirley or me, you will notice we have one thing in common: We both use the gifts we have been given. We both have learned that who we are is who we are intended to be.

And Tom and I now send his shirts to the cleaners. Tom said it's cheaper than replacing them.

The most difficult part of remodeling a home is coming up with a budget.

❧

*C*oming up with the budget for remodeling is no problem. Sticking to the budget—now *that* is the problem. It's easy to say we have x dollars for this home. It's not so easy to go with cheap flooring in the kitchen so we can have tile in the bathroom. Or use a naked bulb over the table so we can have a hardwood floor in the entryway. Or live in three tiny bedrooms so we can have a big garage. Sticking to a budget is the most difficult part. Contrary to popular belief, you don't get what you want when you build your own home, you get what you can afford, which for most people leaves a lot to be desired.

A car is something that should be clean at all times.

❧

ere's why my car is a good car to ride in. Because I carry enough stuff in my car that if we get stuck anywhere away from civilization, we could survive for two weeks without leaving the car. You want blankets? I've got 'em. You want food? I've got it (both used and new). You want shampoo and conditioner? Well, the last time they were on sale, I stocked up, and I have been using my car as a warehouse to store the extras. You want reading material? I have overdue library books and old newspapers and new magazines that just came today. I have books on writing I've been meaning to read and a novel I am halfway through. I've got a first-aid kit and enough makeup to keep a group of flight attendants picture perfect for a week. And candy? Boy, do I have candy. All kinds. Some of it from last Halloween.

So that's why my car is a good car to ride in. Now, my husband's car, on the other hand, is not a good car to ride in. Why? Because he believes that the lie on the previous page is true.

If I ignore it,
it will go away.

～

Evolutionists believe that life evolved into a higher form from chaos. Yes, "from chaos came order," they say. Well, that principle doesn't seem to be true in my everyday life. I have been ignoring things that seem "out of control" for years, and they don't seem to be evolving into something great at all. In fact, in my life the second law of thermodynamics is at work more than the laws of evolution: Things go from order to disorder. And you'd think that since I know that, I wouldn't ignore things and hope they will get better—but still I do. Here are some things I've ignored for years, hoping that one day they will go away:

The mess in my house. I know we don't have a maid,

but I still leave things lying around. I leave beds unmade and floors unmopped—and I hope the mess will just go away. For example, our refrigerator is full of things I've been ignoring, such as dates I recently found that were *a year* past their expiration date and mold on things that you didn't know mold could grow on. I'm thinking of putting a sign on our refrigerator door that says, "Scientific experiment going on—do not disturb." That way, when we have friends over, they will understand why, if they even approach the refrigerator, I fling my body between them and the door, flailing my arms to distract them. I'll point to the sign and tell them that there are things in here that are scary, and only someone who knows about the "mold experiment" would understand the need to keep the door closed. So stay out.

My weight. I know that if you gain only one pound a month, in five years you'll be sixty pounds overweight. I know that because I've gained one pound a month for the last twenty-seven months. But I keep hoping that if I ignore my rear end, it will go away.

The male and female guinea pigs who now live together in one cage. We seriously don't want more guinea pig babies. I'm hoping if I ignore the situation, perhaps those pigs will learn abstinence.

The lack of quality programming on television. I've been angry about the lack of quality programming on TV for years. But ignoring the stuff on TV is easier than protesting, because it's time-consuming to try to bring change to network TV. Maybe if I ignore it, it will go away, and good will come in its place.

But I have noticed that some things really do go away if you ignore them. Health, for example. Every person I've ever known who has ignored her health has one day lost it.

I can do it all.

❧

$\mathcal{I}$ used to think I could be a great writer and a great cook and a great housekeeper and a great wife and an involved mother of a six-year-old. I can't. So I have to choose priorities. In our family what works for us is for me to concentrate on three things: our marriage, our child, and my writing. Everything else falls by the wayside.

Sure, I could cook more if I didn't work all day as a writer. And I could keep a cleaner house if I wasn't committed to regularly taking my daughter someplace fun, like the library, so we can have what we call "girls' days out." But I can't do it all. We pick and choose what is important to us. What works for us may not be the priorities in your family. But nobody does it all—except maybe those women in 1950s sitcoms. They did dress awfully nice just to hang around the house. And they never seemed to argue with their husbands about how much they spent on all those clothes.

Lies I Believed
About Marriage

Planning my wedding would be a joy.

❧

Ever since I was eight years old, I had been thinking about my wedding. I knew it would be a great occasion. I knew that all the days leading up to the wedding would be filled with joy and wonder as we approached this most anticipated event.

But in real life, planning my wedding was not anything like what I had dreamed. It was, instead, the pits. A mess of stress, as I refer to it now.

Maybe it was because I was trying to do it all myself. Or maybe it was because my mother had been ill with cancer and died six weeks before our wedding day. Or maybe it was that we had less than two months to get the whole thing together. Or maybe it was that we were on such a tight budget and I was working overtime on my day job. I just know that the whole thing nearly put me over the edge.

And I'm not alone in this feeling that the wedding planning was not a joyous occasion. I've talked with hundreds of brides who went though the same PWDS I went though. PWDS is Pre-Wedding-Day Stress, and when you mix it with PMS, which is a common malady among women around the world, and then you combine those two with PFB (Post-Flight Behavior), which is common to me as a flight attendant, well, you have something so powerful and potentially explosive that some manufacturers are looking for a way to bottle it.

It wasn't just that the picking of the bridesmaids alone strained lifelong relationships and provided fodder for bitterness among friends and relatives for years to come. It was the choice of fabric for the dresses—"I don't really look good in that color"—and the choice of flowers for the church—"You want that much money for sixty-four roses?"—and then the travel arrangements. Tom and I were living in a town away from family, so where was everyone going to stay when they arrived and could we really ask that many people to fly all that way? Even now, when I think back to all the things we dealt with, I break out into a cold sweat.

But the worst experience about our wedding involved the wedding cake. We had hired a baker from a bakery downtown to bake a cake just like the one he had in the window. We had paid in advance. The day of the wedding, I was informed just before I walked down the aisle that no cake had arrived. "Call them," I hissed. "Beg them to get it here."

Then the music started and I moved forward. But someone was stepping on my train. The headpiece was attached so firmly to my hair that when I lurched forward, not realizing the weight of the person on my train, my neck snapped back as if I were going to do a backbend. Before I could right myself, I heard four-letter words coming out of my mouth and looked up to see the shocked faces of new relatives. Who was this woman Tom was committing himself to? Once I got down the aisle, I half expected a chorus of loud voices when the minister asked if there was anyone who knew any reason why these two should not be joined in matrimony. For weeks afterward I had a recurring nightmare about that moment and dreamed people actually shouted out, "She's a heathen. Don't let him marry a Philistine!"

But the ceremony went on. And we had no more major crises until the cutting of the cake. The cake had arrived, and true to our request, it looked just like the one in the window. In fact, it looked absolutely identical to the one in the window. In fact, as we cut it, or tried to cut it, we realized it *was* the cake from the window.

Apparently the baker had forgotten or misplaced our order. When he got the call just before I walked down the aisle, he found the order, saw that we wanted a cake just like the one in the window, and realized he had no time to bake the cake. So he brought the one from the window.

The funniest part of our wedding video is Tom and I trying to cut that cake. It was, of course, impossible to cut. At least with a knife. A power saw would have done it. But we hacked away and finally began to chip what could be called bite-size pieces. Because we didn't find out the truth until after the wedding, we kept commenting that this was the stalest cake we'd ever seen. We served several pieces, watched people spit it out, and then moved guests on to the nuts and candy. So if you were at my wedding that day and you didn't get a piece of cake, there is a good reason.

When Tom and I got to our hotel that night after our wedding, we both fell on the bed in exhaustion, and Tom said, "I'd rather die than go through that again." I couldn't have agreed more.

When it looks as if my husband is listening, he is.

∽

The year was 1995, and Tom and I didn't yet have a child, so we could use our rides in the car as a time for catching up on serious conversation. I loved those times of sharing with each other because there was nothing to distract us. At home there were phone calls, doorbells, the newspaper, or sports on television. But when we were in the car, nothing could stop our open line of one-to-one heartfelt talks.

Now, when Tom drives, he keeps his eyes on the road. And I'm proud of him for that—it makes me feel he's a safe driver. So I was used to him not looking at me during our car talks.

On this one day in 1995, we were driving down a two-lane road in a small town, and since there was no traffic, I felt even more in Tom's center of attention than I usually do. Since I had a lot of words stored up, I began to talk and found myself sharing some very deep emotions and talking for twenty minutes straight. Tom's body language told me he was really concentrating on what I was saying—in fact, the further I got into my story, the more he seemed intent on his concentration. This encouraged me to talk even more.

Finally I paused and said, "Honey, what do you think of that?" Tom leaned forward, shifted his position as if he were about to say something deep, and with that look of concentration on his face again, said, "I can't believe it."

Well, that told me I had definitely touched an emotional nerve. I was just about to respond to his sensitive reply to my pain, when he spoke again, looking straight ahead and seemingly deeply touched. "Those two cracks have finally come together."

Tom had been concentrating all right—on the two cracks in the windshield, which had begun weeks before on different sides of the car and had now, apparently in an amazing feat, come together.

My mouth dropped open just as the car stopped at

a stop sign. Tom looked over at me and realized his error. "I'm sorry," he said. "What were you saying?"

The intensity of my emotion and the intensity of his concentration were so far removed from each other that we both suddenly burst into laughter at the absurdity of two people trying to communicate on completely different levels.

We laughed for several minutes, and then Tom tried in vain to get me to understand his fascination with those two windshield cracks. And I tried to explain my fascination with emotions and their origins. Suffice it to say, just because your husband appears to be listening doesn't mean he is.

There's nothing
I can do about it.

❧

When Tom and I were first married, we had different ways of arguing. Tom—in a nutshell—wanted to discuss things calmly. And I, well, wanted to yell and scream.

In my family it wasn't always logic that won arguments. Sometimes it was the person who yelled the loudest. Or screamed the longest.

So in one of my first arguments with Tom, I let him have the full brunt of my verbal fury.

And he walked out.

I watched him go out the door and began to scream, "You can't walk out on me. I'm talking to you!" Tom put his head back in the room and said, "When you can talk to me in a civil tone, we will talk.

But I respect myself too much to allow you to address me in that tone. I will not be yelled at." And with that, Tom left the apartment.

I had never in all my life been treated with such—how do you say it?—rudeness. That's what it was. How could he walk out on me? When I was trying to communicate!

Finally, when I had calmed down, Tom came back home and we talked. And Tom explained to me that he would not put up with disrespect in how I related to him or how he related to me. We would respect each other even in our tones when we argued.

I learned a lot that day about how to communicate. And since then, Tom has only reminded me a few times that arguing is not about yelling and that it can be done in calm, respectful tones.

So now I'm a reformed arguer. If I see people in public using the rude, yelling method of communicating, it's all I can do not to approach them and say, "Hey, you know that is being disrespectful, and your spouse doesn't have to put up with it."

But if I start to approach a couple with my reformed-arguer passion, Tom gets up to leave again. He's still working on convincing me that some things just aren't my business.

You can tell what
a couple is arguing about
by listening to their words.

Once, in the first weeks of our married life, I asked Tom to go out and move his car so I could unload some things from the trunk. Tom replied in a tone I didn't like, and I instantly got furious at him and started trying to escalate the situation. At first, Tom tried to defend himself, but then he put his arms around me and said quietly, "What is this really about?" At that moment, I realized that the whole thing upsetting me wasn't what I was articulating but a tiny action of his that reminded me of a moment when I felt out of control as a young child. The emotional trigger was something that Tom had no way of knowing he was repeating—and had no way of knowing I'm not going to address straight on.

So if I were using this moment to tell young married couples a bit of advice—which I am—I'd say, "Look for anger behind the anger when you are arguing." Just listening to the words usually doesn't tell you what is really wrong.

I will never disown
my husband.

❧

Tom and I hadn't been married very long, and I was working three days a week as a flight attendant. Tom used my flight benefits to come with me on some trips. One particular weekend, Tom was exhausted before we even left. He had worked all day, then rushed to the airport, grabbed some dinner, and boarded the plane. I was thrilled he was going with me and so proud of my new handsome husband that I couldn't wait to show him off to the other flight attendants.

About ten minutes after Tom boarded, I noted his seat number and told another flight attendant to go look in the back of the twin-aisle aircraft. Then she could meet the man of my dreams. I told her to look for a handsome dude with a great smile.

She came back and said she couldn't find him.

I walked to the back and stopped. Tom looked like a large bug sprawled in a tight space. One leg was draped over the seat next to him; his head was back and his mouth wide open, with a toothpick lying on his lower lip. He was snoring, and when he breathed in, the toothpick moved up, and when he breathed out, the toothpick moved down. I noticed that from this angle the David Letterman–type gap between his front teeth was prominent. I stared at him and then turned and walked back into first class.

On the way, I met the flight attendant who had wanted to meet Tom, World's Handsomest Man.

"Where is he?" she asked. "I want to see him. Did you find him?"

I looked her straight in the eye and said, "He didn't get on yet."

Just when you think you'll never deny the one you love, you do. Sometimes fear of public humiliation wins over commitment.

My husband will
love my advice.

J had heard that most men don't like unsolicited
advice. The book *Men Are from Mars, Women
Are from Venus* says that men think unsolicited
advice is an insult—as in "I know what I am doing,
and I don't need your advice." Whereas, women think
advice is a sign of love—as in "Thank you for caring
enough to share your opinion of what is best."

I thought my husband would not be like the cave-
men described in the book. I thought he would be
enlightened enough to recognize my unsolicited advice
for what it was—a sign of my love.

So for the first sixteen years of our marriage, I gave
Tom advice on everything, from how he drives to how

he makes the lunch for our daughter to how he mows the lawn.

And for most of our married life, he ignored me, but I figured he was quietly cherishing what I said. Then came the one shocking day when he obviously *didn't* cherish it. When he went nuts over it, and I don't mean for joy.

My husband is normally quiet and sweet and unruffled. That's why God put us together, because *quiet* and *sweet* and *unruffled* are not words used to describe me. Ever. But back to the day Tom went nuts.

It happened in a basketball game that Tom was coaching. He was doing very well, but I thought—after a few minutes—that he must not have noticed the one player who had been on the sidelines a minute too long, and so I tried to get Tom's attention from my seat near the side of the court. When I realized he was either ignoring me or was blind, I decided he would never ignore me, so he must be blind—in one eye or something. You know, all that sweat could blind his vision. So I tiptoed out to the middle of the court where he stood with a whistle in his mouth, and I tugged on his shirt-sleeve. When he didn't turn right away, I tugged harder.

Well, I'm here to tell you, if you have ever seen that Hulk on television, where the mild-mannered guy turns into something fierce, with veins and muscles popping out, that is exactly what happened to my husband. He turned to me and screamed, "GET OFF THE COURT!" Then he followed me back to my seat, yelling, "DO YOU THINK I DON'T KNOW WHAT I'M DOING?!" Which was totally stupid—of course I knew he knew what he was doing. That's why he was the coach, because he knew what he was doing. But I thought for sure he'd realize two heads are better than one.

Well, apparently not...in coaching.

Later, after we talked about the incident, I came to the sad realization that my husband was just like those other men who didn't like advice. He explained to me that the only way he could interpret my walking out on that court was that I thought he didn't know what he was doing. And I told him the only way I could interpret my advice was that I loved him and wanted to offer him the best shot at the whole picture, from my angle.

I told him his behavior had embarrassed me. And he said my behavior had embarrassed him—as if every woman there wouldn't have done the same for her husband.

Well, it turns out every woman there was equally stunned that I had walked onto the court in the middle of a game. "Marsha, there are some things we just know, and one of them is, you don't interrupt a game your husband is coaching to give him advice from the sidelines. Everyone knows that." Well, apparently not everyone.

Lies I Believed About Children

With enough organization, I can control my child.

◦～๑

I know it's an old saying: Those who don't have children are experts at raising them. And I was no different—before I had a child, I told anyone who would listen that if parents just exercised enough organization and control, they could have a nearly perfect child. And then I had a child and found there are certain things you can't control.

The most recent example of this came after I spent the morning preparing six-year-old Mandy to have her picture taken by a professional photographer. I wanted her hair perfect, her dress clean and pressed, her shoes polished.

Every action that morning was geared to keeping her perfect until we were in that car and headed the short distance to the photographer. I didn't let her eat in her dress. I didn't let her bounce around after the curlers came out of her hair. She couldn't go near her shoes until the last minute. Finally the moment came, and I sent her dressed, coifed, and spotless to the car as I turned to lock our front door.

When I got to the car, Mandy wasn't there. When I called for her, she came running around the corner with a look of pride on her face. She was filthy but glowing.

I was so stunned by her appearance and the expression on her face that I could barely get my words out. "Where…did…you…go?"

"Oh," she said, waving her hand, "I just went to say good-bye to the dog. And"—she paused—"did you know Angel and I can both fit in her doghouse?"

I have a rule that it's not a good thing to yell at my daughter. I could see that she didn't understand that she had just unraveled hours of tightly woven organization. I calmly explained that this was a big problem for me and told her we were out of time. Now we had to change her clothes. We headed back into the house to put on the second-best dress for the pictures.

We washed mud off her legs, arms, and face and combed golden retriever fur out of her hair. Then we changed her clothes, polished her shoes again, and I said, "This time I'm going to the car first, and you are *not* to say good-bye to the dog. I'm locking the front door, so just turn the lock on the back door and get to the car. We're running late."

I don't know why I said the word *running,* but it must have put an idea into her head. Mandy probably figured if we were running late, she'd run to the car. So she did, and I looked up just in time to watch her right foot land firmly into a large pile of golden retriever excrement. It must have been fresh excrement, because it splashed and splattered everywhere.

I put my head down on the steering wheel and began making the low guttural sound of a wounded organizational leader. With grit all over her, my daughter walked to the driver's side window and said, "Sorry, Mommy."

We headed back into the house for a third cleaning. No matter how much you try, some things, like childlike impulse and where little feet land, are not controlled by organization.

A child is the glue that holds a marriage together.

❧

I've heard couples say, "Well, we're not getting along right now, but I think after the baby is born, we'll really be close." Tom and I realized this was a lie right after Mandy was born.

We had a strong marriage before our baby was born, and in many ways having Mandy *has* brought us closer together. But I have to tell you: What we had thought would be the romantic glow of new parenthood turned out to be a dim glare of no sleep. And the light was harsh.

We had the baby and suddenly we realized we were slaves. Although we were slaves of love, we were on duty 24/7.

The stress of no sleep and this new huge responsibility produced arguments over a whole new set of issues—like whose life was the most affected by this change. And then there were the hormonal changes in my personality immediately following Mandy's birth. It seemed to me that Tom had suddenly changed from a brilliant rocket scientist to someone who obviously didn't know how to do anything right. He couldn't change the baby correctly or bathe her without my criticism. He couldn't say the right things to me when I was depressed—which was for a full six weeks after she was born. And he couldn't get close to me at all because I had eyes only for the baby. As far as I was concerned, he could go live on another planet.

Of course, this all changed as the baby got older. Except the sleep part. We still are sleep-deprived. But give us a few more years. I mean, she's only six.

Tom likes now to say, "If marriage is an experience in self-sacrifice, having a baby is a graduate course." And self-sacrifice is usually in short supply in most marriages. So if you think a baby will hold your marriage together, I am sorry to tell you, that's just not the truth.

My child will never do that.

efore I became a parent, I had been warned not to say, "My child will never do that." But I knew my child truly would never do certain things—like break prized possessions or run wild in a store or act like a maniac when I was introducing her to someone important to my career.

The truth is she has done all those things and more, and I'm thinking now that children provide great humor in heaven, as God watches them bring humility into the lives of their parents. At least that's what raising our daughter has done for me.

It's going to be
our daughter's pet.

❧

*I*f it's my daughter's pet, why am I the one who is home with it all day, making sure it gets water and food and play toys? And taking it to the vet? And making sure the neighbor kids don't get bitten by it? If this pet is my daughter's, why do I have most of the responsibility for it? Because folks, if your daughter is six years old and goes to school every day, the cold truth is the pet is Mom's. Mom will be the one caring for it.

I've decided that until kids are nine or ten and can take complete care of their menagerie, without prompting, whatever pet they bring home is actually not a pet but a responsibility for Mom. I didn't say the truth was pretty; I'm just telling it like it is.

I will never argue with my kids—they will just obey me.

❦

efore I was a parent, I would tell you all the things I would do right when I became a parent, and I would mention one thing I knew I would never do: argue with a six-year-old. I mean, I am an adult. I would be Mom. What I said would be law. You don't question the law, especially if you are in first grade. Right? There *is* such a thing as discipline, after all. Well, I'm embarrassed to admit I have argued with my daughter on many an occasion. Even my husband has argued with her. I've heard him say, "I'm not going to argue with you," meaning, of course, he is already engaged in an argument.

So all I'm trying to tell you here is you think you will have a perfectly run home with no back-talk from your children, and then you hit real life. You do the best you can, read all the books, and pray it all works out. But in reality, I think I need a bumper sticker that says: "Back-talk happens."

Lies I Believed About Money

No, really, I want to get the check.

❧

My family had a policy that I didn't think was unique to us. Until I tried it with my husband's parents. The policy in my family was that at the end of a dinner out together, we would all argue over the check. None of us meant what we said. But it was sort of a verbal ballet, played out in our family to save face for those of us who couldn't afford to pay.

It went like this: One of us would look at the check and say, "Let me get it." Because everyone understood what was to happen next, a second person would then say, "No, let me get the check." And then a third person would insist on getting the check. The argument would go on and on, escalating in volume and enthusiasm until it came back to me, and I would say, "No, really, I want to get the check." Which, of course, everybody knew was my way of trying to save face. Eventually, the person at the table with the best-paying job (of the year) would reach over, grab the check, and over our loud, false protestations, gloriously pay the bill. Now, of course, I thought all families had this routine—until the weekend I met Tom's parents, Bob and Shirley.

Bob, Shirley, Tom, and I were having lunch at a nice restaurant. The check arrived, and as Bob reached for it, I started my usual vigorous protestations. "Please, please, I'd like to get the check." Tom's father looked at Tom's mother, and Tom looked at me, then Tom's parents who are ever-gracious and never argue in public—with anyone—simply said, "Okay."

I was stunned. There was no volley. There were no protestations. There was not one mention from anyone of "No, let me." Did these people not know the rules of life? Were they being rude? On purpose? What in the name of decency was wrong with them?

There was no way I could afford this.

As everyone started to get up from the table, I weakly grabbed the check and used my rent money to cover the lunch bill.

I never again offered to pay for any meal that I didn't have the money to pay for. I had known there was this verse in the Bible that said let your yes be yes and your no be no. But I didn't realize anyone took that literally—especially at restaurants.

Credit cards bring freedom.

The problem with this lie is that it's true in the beginning. Then the bill comes, and it's more than I can pay. And I don't have anyone to pay it for me. And then I am a slave to the pain and fear and embarrassment of debt.

I heard somewhere that crack dealers give away the first sample: "Here, take a trip for free." And then the people come back for more.

I think credit cards are like that. You can be seduced in the beginning, but you're a slave later.

"There is pleasure in sin for a season." I wonder if the guy who wrote that had a Visa card.

Money will shield
us from pain.

❦

J have a friend who drives a Mercedes, and her husband drives a Lexus. Their home was featured in *Better Homes and Gardens*. It is a perfect example of a very expensive show home. The husband worked as a partner for a large law firm. The wife was involved in charitable activities. They had it all. Even two beautiful sons spaced perfectly, two years apart.

Then one day, their youngest son died. He was only five months old. He lay down for his nap and never woke up. His death was diagnosed as sudden infant death syndrome. The pain of that death has never ended for this family. They have gone on to have other children, but the baby who left their family early is spoken of often. And each year, at the time when he died, they know fresh pain and fresh hurt.

I used to look at that family and think, "Money buys perfection." But it doesn't. A perfect world would be one in which there is no pain. And all the riches we can earn can't buy that world.

It's a good idea to hide
the mail so my husband
won't be depressed when
he sees the bills.

❧

This is the kind of story you'll read and say, "How could you be so stupid?" I don't know. I just was, okay? I'm just telling the truth here, and sometimes telling the truth means admitting things you are not proud of and you would never do again.

It was in the beginning of our marriage, and I noticed my husband had a tendency to get depressed when he opened up a credit card bill and found we didn't have the money to pay it. So I thought, *I'll hide the bills. Then he won't be so depressed.* That worked only for one month. Then we got a late notice, and Tom was a lot more depressed than he would have been if he had gotten the original bill. At least, that was what he said.

After that I didn't *mean* to hide the bills, but they often got lost in my car somewhere, which is sort of like getting lost in the Grand Canyon, only messier. So after that we made a deal that he would be the one who got the mail, not me. I'm not gifted in keeping track of small things like letters and envelopes. Hey, I'm only telling the truth here.

Lies I Believed About People and Relationships

It's not enough to listen to someone who has a problem. I need to try to fix it.

Sometimes just having someone listen is enough. I heard a story once about a woman who ran an ad in the paper that said, "Will listen without judgment or comment." She put her phone number in the paper and charged fifty dollars per hour.

She was deluged with calls.

I have someone like this woman in my life. And I never expected her to be there. My listener is my editor. And, no, you can't have her phone number. When I'm working on a book with her, we don't just talk about the book. Sometimes I call her with complaints like how difficult it is to be a writer. And how every time I sit down at the computer, the house starts screaming at me to clean it. And how when I try to finish a book, it never fails but everyone in the family gets sick and needs to visit the doctor and needs me to drive. Including our three pets.

While I was writing my last book, the fish didn't make it, which, of course, called for time out for a funeral. Our guinea pig, Princess I, died from my feeding her cold lettuce. (Who knew?) As of this writing, we have a new guinea pig, Princess II, who recently gave birth to three more guinea pigs. Which we had to wean after just the right number of days and then immediately adopt out because they were boys. (And quite frankly those guinea pig boys were acting like animals!)

And then there was the whole training of our golden retriever, and well, there's too much to go into here. Suffice it to say, my editor listens to everything, and she makes proper empathetic sounds and says (since she is also a writer) that she can understand and that she has had the same "writer's lament" experiences of juggling work, family, and time.

And she heals me with her listening.

Having someone listen to you is wonderfully therapeutic. But don't tell my editor; she might start charging.

Going public about a wrong you have suffered is a good way to get justice.

❦

J have a dear friend whom we will call J. She worked as a real estate saleswoman for a large developer.

The developer misappropriated several thousand dollars of funds from the buyers and essentially didn't give my friend her commission on her sales. But J didn't sue. She just left and went to another company because, she said, "This is a town where everyone in this business knows someone in this business. So even if I won, I would lose, because I would end up the one who was labeled a troublemaker and never work again in the same field. People don't hire someone who made trouble for her former employer."

Sometimes going public about someone who has wronged you backfires, and the evil you are trying to expose splashes back on you.

There is a time and a place for public exposure— and a time and a place to remember the Bible verse that says vengeance belongs to God.

No one will know I'm in love.

Love by its very nature is expressive. It cannot be squelched. That, I am convinced, is why a band of twelve men was able to change the world. They changed the world because of love for one rabbi who had captured their hearts. One teacher they could not get over. One man who they said was who he said he was.

They were so in love with this teacher that nothing was going to shut them up. They had never met someone like him. Even after they are all dead and gone, their love for this guy still speaks, because the stories they wrote down were copied word for word by scribes and teachers over and over again, century after century.

Love propagated Christianity. Because love by its very nature is expressive.

Kindness makes a guy wimpy.

Kindness makes a man attractive. For years I've watched some of the most attractive women in the world marry guys who weren't —how shall I say this?—the epitome of handsome. I kept wondering how these guys ended up with these babes.

Then I realized all those guys had one thing in common: They were kind. And I realized that kindness makes a guy attractive. At least to supermodels and flight attendants. I've seen it happen time and time again. So if you are not the most attractive guy in the world, try kindness. Practice it as if it were an art. You will attract the attention of beautiful women. I can guarantee it. Because kindness makes a guy look much better than lifting weights does. I've seen it with my own eyes.

Men who drive flashy cars are more desirable than men who drive plain cars.

I like to tell people it was my husband's car that drew me to him. Because it was. But, lest they assume Tom drove a flashy car, I set them straight. It was the fact that he *didn't* have a flashy car that made me love him. Tom was out of college a few years when I met him. He had no debt. He could drive any kind of car he wanted. And he chose a lower-priced, solid, practical car. One that got good mileage and still had a sunroof, for fun. Tom's choice of a car said to me, *This man is secure in who he is.* He didn't need a manhood-magnifier car that some men have to feel more like a man.

I had always been looking for a man who was so secure that he didn't need to drive something that made him feel as if he were something he wasn't. I found that man in Tom.

So it's true. It was Tom's car that attracted me to him.

I will never fall in love with someone who is nothing but sweet talk.

My only consolation with this story is that I was young, desperate, and vulnerable. I'd just broken off a long-term relationship and was standing in Walgreens reading *Bride's* magazine, figuring I'd never have a happy life, when I heard an incredible male voice. Now, you can tell a lot about a man by his tone of voice. And this guy was the kindest, most genuine-sounding guy I'd ever heard. It seemed like a good idea to track down the man to whom the voice belonged.

It was so noisy in the store that I could only hear parts of his conversations, such as "Thank you!"

"Come again!" and "May I help you?" He seemed to be saying, "May I help you?" to every person who came up to him, in fact. Now, how great is that! He obviously wasn't chewing gum and making jokes with his fellow employees. This guy was kind *and* conscientious.

While I was following the sound of his voice and trying to sneak a peak at my new love, I was mentally making a list of his good qualities. Work ethic: obviously good. Kindness: good. Treating everyone with the same consideration: good. This guy probably came from a great family who had instilled in him great values.

After a few minutes I found him. I just turned one last corner, and there he was standing by the door, surrounded by customers who appeared as charmed as I was. He didn't exactly look like the man of my dreams. I mean, he was tall and built like a steel truck...but...

I just figured we would make it work. The fact that I was in love with the talking Coca-Cola machine at Walgreens would be nobody's business but my own.

I'd like to tell you I stopped it right there. I'd like to say that I never went back to that machine after the humiliating first meeting, but I did. I'd like to say that I didn't spend nights counting out stacks of quarters, days dreaming of our potential future meetings...but, I did. And I'd like to say, this didn't go on for more than a week. But I'd be lying.

Finally the ugly truth hit me; I could ignore it no longer. I was in love with someone who was tall and flashy looking but who, quite frankly, didn't care about me at all. And would never be a good father to our children.

He just said whatever he could to get people to love him. And when the attention wasn't on him, he became quite sullen. That's why I broke up with him.

Although I eventually recovered from tall-dark-and-handsome-vendor love, I still think of him on occasion. Especially when I'm in airports and see others who look like him—though none can match that melodic voice.

We should withhold
good things from people
who have done us wrong.
That will teach them a lesson.

One of the most interesting concepts of the
Bible is the one about doing good to those
who have done us wrong. Not repaying evil
for evil. I suppose if you really want to teach your ene-
mies a lesson, you would love them as you love yourself. That could teach the whole world a thing or two.

People who are reserved cannot be funny.

<figure>❧</figure>

My husband is a very reserved man and yet one of the funniest men I know. He is a master of one-liners.

Once Tom and I were being interviewed by a reporter for a magazine. The reporter talked to me for most of an hour, while I bubbled over with all kinds of funny stories. And Tom, in his usual stance, was quiet, simply enjoying the show.

Finally the interviewer turned to him and found out that he was an aerospace engineer and that his mother was a nurse and his father a pharmacist and that they had all been born and raised in a conservative Midwest environment. "Well," began the interviewer, trying to sum up my relationship to Tom's relatives, "after hearing about your parents, I can bet Marsha must just be like opening a window for them and letting in a breath of fresh air."

Tom looked her in the eye and said, "I'm not sure they like that much breeze."

Busy people don't like to be interrupted.

~~~~

It was June 2003, and I was busier than I'd been in ages. First of all, it was summer so my daughter wasn't in school. She did go to a day camp for a few hours a day, and while she was gone, I frantically worked on a book that was due. This busy, pressured feeling was complicated by the fact that my second book had been out only for a few days, so I also had a publicity campaign going on—a campaign made unique by the fact that I was taking my six-year-old with me to book signings and television interviews.

I was grinding my teeth at night from tension. And when I was home during the day, I was working so hard at the computer that my neck hurt. Trying to write something that is easy to read is not an easy task for me.

At this time in my life, if you had asked me if busy people like to be interrupted, I would have told you, "*No,* they *do not* like to be interrupted."

But then I met someone delightful. She came into a store where I was doing a book signing, and we chatted briefly. And we made plans to get together. This eventually led to lunch and to a few e-mail exchanges.

In her second e-mail, my new friend began apologizing for "bugging" me when she knew I was so busy.

Before I answered that e-mail, I realized this woman was such a refreshing spirit that after just a few weeks of knowing her, I cherished her friendship. So I wrote back to her and said, "A bug is a gnat. You are a butterfly, and what do people do when they get a chance to see a butterfly up close? They stop and catch a glimpse of awe and thank God for this moment of beauty. And moments like that are even more precious to people who are busy."

So the truth is, if someone is very busy and she finds a gnat buzzing around with nothing to offer but noise and irritation, then that someone who is busy will not want to be interrupted. But if she catches a glimpse of a butterfly that is gentle in the landing and lovely in the visit—she will gladly stop everything for a closer look.

You don't say no
to people you love.

~~9)

*Y*ou love yourself, don't you? And yet you say no to yourself every day. When you want to jump across the desk in your boss's office, grab him by the collar of his starched shirt, and say, "Give me a raise or get out!" you don't say that. You say no to yourself. Or what about in the movie theater when the guy behind you is talking and you've already given him The Look. You don't stand up and say, "Go ahead, make my day!" because you know that is not a good thing for you to do. You say no to yourself and might even leave the movie theater.

Or what about when the guy with the car that cost more than your mother's house parks his piece of flash sideways across the only two parking spaces left at the doctor's office? He is, of course, just asking for someone to take tempera paints to the side of his car and write, "Nice parking job, buddy," but you don't do that either. Or what about the time you wanted to dive into a chocolate cake, face first? These are all times when you have said no to yourself. And in some ways you love yourself more than you love anyone.

Maybe you haven't ever wanted to do any of these things, but I have. I say no to myself a hundred times a day—when my body begs me to call in sick to work or when my mind suggests it would be a good idea to run a red light, for example. So the truth is, we say no to people we love every day. And that is why the world is as peaceful a place as it is, because every day most people say no constantly—to the one they love most.

Things are more important than people.

❦

hen I was a teenager, I attended a youth group at a local church. The youth pastor's name was Larry, and his wife was Ruth Ann. Larry and Ruth Ann probably have no idea that the biggest lesson I learned from them was not taught in the church. It was not one sermon or one Sunday-school lesson. The biggest lesson I learned from Larry and Ruth Ann is that people are more important than things.

I am absent-minded on the best of days, but when I was a teenager, I was even more scattered than I am now. When Larry and Ruth Ann loaned me their best record album, I loved it and treated it with care and then put it in my car to return to them and accidentally left the car in the hot California sun. The record melted.

When I returned the warped record, begging forgiveness, Larry said, "People are more important than things. We'll get over the loss of this thing."

Then I borrowed one of their two halves of a zip-together sleeping bag. I left it in my car, unlocked, overnight. I lived in a bad area and someone stole it. When I went to Larry and Ruth Ann and said, "I'm so sorry," they said, "People are more important than things. You're a person. We value you more than that sleeping bag."

They never brought it up again. And the list goes on and on. I accidentally broke, ruined, or lost numerous things of theirs, and through it all, in the entire four years I knew them, the answer was, "Marsha, people are more important than things."

I would never have learned that lesson by someone telling me—I had to benefit from a live message.

Today, when I think of Larry and Ruth Ann, I don't remember any Bible stories they told me. What I remember is their legacy: People are more important than things.

People will know
I'm exaggerating.

❧

I come from a family of storytellers. Everyone in my family competed to tell the funniest story. Hyperbole, or exaggeration for the use of emphasis, was a part of our storytelling. If we wanted to say the person wasn't feeling well, we said, "He was dying, ya know what I mean, the guy was dying." And, of course, everyone knew this meant that the guy didn't feel well. Or if we wanted to say something was repeated often, we would say, "I'm not joking, the guy said that one hundred times, okay?" This means the guy said it maybe five times—at most.

We knew our family language, and I thought the communication used in our family was universal.

That is until I met Tom's family.

Tom was born and raised in the conservative Midwest. His mother was a nurse; his father was a pharmacist. These are not careers for the inexact. They both made straight A's in college.

But when I first met Bob and Shirley, they didn't seem that odd. It took a full day for me to realize that hyperbole not only was not a part of their lives, it was an anathema to them.

My first glimpse of this came as Tom and I returned from my first Big Red football game. The Huskers were wonderful and I was excited. I walked into the kitchen and took off my winter coat and half yelled, "Wow! There must have been a million people there. The stadium was packed!"

Shirley stopped cooking, turned to Bob, and said, "Bob, that stadium only holds seventy-six thousand, doesn't it?" Then her brow furrowed as if she was trying to figure out if I was a pathological liar or just strange.

This little encounter should have been a clue to me to be quiet. But I didn't get that clue, so I marched on: "Whoa! Was it cold out there! It was like eighty below zero—I was freezing!"

Again, Shirley stopped cooking and turned to Bob. "Bob, it's twenty-four degrees outside right now, isn't it?"

Later, we were all around the dinner table, and Bob was telling a story. It became increasingly clear to me that it is very important for Shirley to have the truth of the story down to the exact specifics. Bob would say, "We left at 7:45 to get the Barnells."

And Shirley would say, "Bob, it was 7:50. I looked at the clock."

Then Bob and Shirley would discuss who had looked at the clock last, and Bob would continue. "We drove four blocks and turned left…"

"Bob," Shirley would gently correct him, "it was three blocks. If you count that first block as one, and the last one you can't count because they live on the corner, it was three blocks."

This type of storytelling was lost on me. I couldn't believe I had met someone who thought details were more important than the entertainment value. And I'm sure Shirley and Bob couldn't believe their only son was marrying someone who couldn't get a story right if her life depended on it.

I have since learned that exaggeration for the use of emphasis is known to be a trait of people like me who were born in California and raised on the West Coast, and it is not common to people born and raised in Lincoln, Nebraska.

Lies I Believed About God

You find weird people
only in church.

❧

Without a doubt, my most endearing friendships are with those who have the same value system as I do. And for the most part, I've found those friends in church. Or writers conferences—these are also good places for kindred spirits.

On the other hand, I do have to say that some of the *weirdest* people I have ever met, I have met in church and at writers conferences. So, the truth is, you don't find weird people only in church—you find them at writers conferences as well.

God will never give us more than we can handle.

God will always give us more than we can handle so we'll turn to him for help. Most people turn to God only when they are overwhelmed and at the end of their rope. So in a way, God's giving us more than we can handle could be seen as an attention-getting ploy.

If I love God, I will never
accuse him of leaving me.

I suppose no one loved God more than Jesus did.
And yet, it was he who said, "My God, my God,
why have you forsaken me?"

I can't go to church
because of all the hypocrites.

~~~~~

I've always thought it interesting that some people claim they don't want to go to church because of all the hypocrites who go there. The fact is we deal with hypocrites all day long, everywhere.

Take your job, for example. Don't you work with some people who claim to be the boss's best friends and then bad-mouth him behind his back? Or what about people who are running for public office? Have you ever seen someone promise to do one thing once she is elected, then do another thing entirely?

Hypocrisy is everywhere. It's part of living in a world that's not perfect.

And besides, Jesus worshiped in a church full of hypocrites. It didn't stop him from being close to God. It shouldn't stop me either.

God helps those
who help themselves.

*G*od helps those who *cannot* help themselves. Every day there are those who say, "I can't do this alone." And they look up and receive what it takes to go on.

Those who never look up never see the light.

God can't use
broken things.

⌒〜⌒

roken things are actually what God loves and
holds close to himself. Broken hearts. Broken
dreams. Sick people, broken people. These
are the things most treasured by the One who didn't
come to save those who are well but those who are sick.

A broken and a contrite heart, God will not
despise.

Lies I Believed About Appearances

No one will notice.

❧

*Y*ears ago, my hair—at least some of my hairs—decided to lose its natural color and go gray. I was stunned that this obvious sign of old age should happen to me at such a young age. I wasn't even married yet. How gauche.

With the appearance of the first gray, I began the long journey of trial and error to find a way to get rid of it. Now, the reason I say trial and error is because there have been some major errors with what I have tried.

I won't go into all the stories of all the failures. Instead, I'll tell you just one. The one that happened last week.

I had purchased some spray-on color. It was used by kids who wanted to put streaks in their hair for Halloween. I thought it might also be good for my roots, right at my temple, which I like to be the color of warm cinnamon or honey. Not the color of snow.

I knew this spray stuff was water soluble, so I was going to use it only on a day when it wasn't raining. I waited until a beautiful August day and got myself all dressed up for my husband. I had on my best outfit. My hair was perfect—I'd styled it and I sprayed the temples.

Tom and I walked out to the car and stopped to talk to a neighbor. The sun was beating down on us, and we were having a good time when I noticed Tom looking at me closely. I thought he was admiring the way I looked, so I ran my hand along my face and stood in what I thought was a graceful pose.

The neighbor went back to her home, and Tom kept staring at my head. "What is wrong with your face?" he said.

"Nothing. Why do you ask?"

"Because you have been in the dirt or something."

I grabbed a mirror and saw that the color I had sprayed on my temples was running down my face in little sweat lines. My coy hand movement had spread it all over my chin.

Suddenly I realized that sweat was water. My sweat

was making the color run. I looked a mess. Like a half-dipped caramel apple.

If everything that is hidden will one day be made known, we're going to be seeing a lot of things people thought no one would notice. It will be comforting in a way: I'll find out I'm not the only one who had gray hair.

If it looks like garbage,
it must be garbage.

෴

O ne of my favorite stories from our marriage has to do with a dress I bought. It was a lovely formal evening gown. I discovered it one day while walking with Mandy in her stroller and admiring clothes at the designer clearance basement shop. Its tag said the original price was about one month's salary for us. The final markdown—with a no-return/as-is tag and with a tear in the side of the dress that was easily repairable—was $15.95. I just love to get a good deal. Sometimes I've been known to buy things not my size just because they were such a good deal. But this one was definitely my size.

I went into the big dressing room to try it on. It fit perfectly, and as I turned and saw my reflection in the three-way mirror, the years melted away and dreams came forth. I was Cinderella. Only I was a literary Cinderella about to accept the Pulitzer Prize for fiction. I had written a novel that was being reviewed as *"Anna Karenina* meets *A Confederacy of Dunces."* Yes, I was Tolstoy, and I was the guy who killed himself before his talent was revealed. My novel was deep, humorous, and literary. And people around the world were reading it in droves.

I saw them, in crowds, each person holding up the book, reading portions, laughing out loud, thinking deep thoughts, and mentally redefining good literature. Just as one fan gently touched my arm to get my attention, I came back to the present and realized it was actually the salesclerk in the store. "Hellooooo! Do ya want it or not?"

I waved to my fans, my readership, and took my statue (do they give a statue for the Pulitzer?), then went back in the dressing room and removed the gown. Yes, I wanted it. It would be my "dream of someday" gown. It would be the gown that would motivate me and keep me going. And it would be a ball gown that we would use on the one cruise we had ever signed up for.

Which was to happen in just one week. We had

signed up for this cruise because it was dirt cheap for airline personnel, and it was to Alaska, and we loved Alaska, and we could fly home free from Anchorage.

So I had the evening wear for the one black-tie dinner on board the ship.

Soon I had paid my $15.95 and was carrying the gown to my car. Now, if you knew how I keep my car, you would cringe at the thought of a gown like that even entering an area that contained spilled fast food from last week and sticky juice boxes thrown around by my then two-year-old daughter.

But never fear. I was prepared.

I carry in my car a box of large black plastic garbage bags, in case I ever decide to get "out of character" and clean the thing out. It hasn't happened yet, but it could. And the very fact that I keep garbage bags in the car is a great encouragement to my husband. Who we have already established is a rather neat engineer type. And who for those reasons won't let me near his car.

So, because I was prepared, I grabbed a clean black garbage bag and stuffed the perfect dream dress into the garbage bag. And to further ensure it would never be touched by even the smell of old food in the car, I tied the top of the clean, just-unfolded garbage bag in a large tight knot. I even went the further step of pulling up to a gas station and cleaning out every smelly hamburger or old carton of milk or juice—even all the old candy bars—from my car. I didn't want my dress to be in the same room as old stinky things.

When Mandy and I got home from our trip to the store, she was asleep, so I pulled her out of her car seat and, instead of going in the front door, went up the stairs to our back porch and set the bag inside the covered porch by the back door. I didn't want to risk setting the bag inside because I was afraid if I brought it inside the house or left it anywhere but on our covered porch, my husband would see it and think it was garbage and throw it out.

Tom had a business meeting that night, and the next day he had a breakfast meeting so I didn't get to talk to him until the next afternoon, when he got home, and then I told him how excited I was about the dress. The gown of my dreams.

He appeared genuinely excited for me. "Where is it? Go try it on for me."

I went out to the covered back porch and looked by the door, and it wasn't there. I searched all over the porch.

Finally I called to Tom. "Honey, did you see that

black bag out here, with a knot in it? I set it here just yesterday."

"Oh yeah," he said, "When I went out this morning, it was there, and the garbage truck was downstairs, so I grabbed it and just threw it right in the back of that truck. I figured it must be really smelly stuff, because you didn't even want it near the house."

I sat down on the floor in shock. "I had my dress in there," I said in a really small voice. And then I lay down and started crying. "It was my perfect dress!"

"Well, then why did you put it in a garbage bag?"

"I didn't want to get it dirty."

"You should never have put it in a garbage bag."

"You should have looked inside!"

Sometimes if it looks like garbage on the outside, we need to know that there is a treasure inside—if someone could just untie the knot and look in.

If I act the right way, no one will think I'm a fool.

You can never avoid being thought a fool. No matter what you do or how you do it, someone, somewhere, is going to call you a fool. If you are conservative, the liberals will think you are a fool. If you are liberal, the other side, at least part of the time, will think you are a fool. If you are outgoing, some will think you are a buffoon and a fool. If you are quiet, some will think you are a mute fool. If you ride Harleys, the street-bike people will think you are a fool, and if you ride street bikes, the Harley people will laugh at you.

You will always be thought a fool by someone. The question is, whose fool do you want to be?

Criticizing someone else will make me look better.

∽

When Tom and I were dating, we both lived in Los Angeles. Tom lived in Manhattan Beach, and I lived in a cheaper part of town. We had been seeing each other only a few weeks when his parents flew in from Lincoln, Nebraska, to visit their only son. And I, wanting to please Tom, agreed to pick them up at the airport, sight unseen. Tom's father was going to take us all out to lunch. Tom was going to meet us at the restaurant.

To say I was nervous would be an understatement.

I have a history of doing stupid things when I'm nervous. (Okay, I have a history of doing stupid things when I'm not nervous, but when I'm really nervous, I do stupider things. Or maybe just regular stupid things more often.) Now, at the time, Tom was sharing his home with another engineer. He didn't know this guy very well, but he knew enough to figure out that they didn't share the same value system when it came to impressing people.

For example, Tom hated the fact that someone would buy a certain car or certain accessories just for the name recognition. Tom had spent a few of his teenage years living in Grosse Pointe, Michigan, and had gathered from that experience a disdain for anything that smacked of being remotely ostentatious. And when that display was purchased on credit, it bothered Tom all the more. It's bad enough that you need to impress the world with what you own, he would say. It's doubly bad if you can't afford the impression you're making.

To impress Tom, I completely agreed with his philosophy on this. Fully intending to one day adopt it as my own.

So, with this in mind, when his parents finished lunch, I thought I'd impress them by criticizing Tom's friend.

"You won't believe this," I said, "but he had to have a Rolex. I mean a four-thousand-dollar Rolex! How stupid is that? I mean, to spend four thousand on a watch!" I reached for a piece of bread and waved it around to make my point. "Four thousand dollars on one watch. What kind of fool would do that?"

It seemed everyone at the table was stunned at the depth of my remark because they were all quiet. I congratulated myself on saying just the right thing. Then all eyes went to Tom's father, Bob, as he reached across the table so his coat sleeve pulled back. It revealed a large gold watch.

"This is a Rolex," he said.

In the next seconds it seemed I could hear the sound of the blood draining from my face. I had the sinking feeling that this relationship was over. Then, in a desperate attempt to get the attention off my last comment, I said, "Yes, but you didn't buy that on credit, now did you?"

"Noooo," his father and mother said in unison, as if I had suggested they carried a social disease. "We bought it while we were on vacation in Switzerland."

And then, with one sentence Bob, not only took the attention off my prior statement but told me more about himself than I have ever learned about a person in a single sentence.

"It wasn't keeping accurate time when I first got

it," he said, pointing to his watch. "It was losing a second a week."

I spit my coffee across the table in a guffaw and then realized he was serious. No one else was laughing. I coughed and, with an effort that could have won me an Academy Award, stuffed down the laughter that threatened to reveal that this was the weirdest thing I had ever heard.

I was more than interested in this comment—I was dumbfounded. So I asked with genuine curiosity, "How could you tell?"

His parents looked at me as if that was an unnecessary question.

"I noted the time," said his father.

I realized at that moment that Tom's father had added new meaning to the phrase *like clockwork*.

You would think that after almost ruining my relationship with Tom, I would learn not to put people down in public. And I wish I could say you were right.

But no, I still had lots to learn about this. Some people take a long time to outlive lies they thought were true.

If I look like I belong
somewhere, I belong there.

❧

A friend of mine was organizing a benefit for one of the performing arts centers in San Diego, California. Now, Tom and I had never attended a benefit before—our entertainment usually consists of staying home with rented movies and microwave popcorn. But, at the last minute, my friend needed to fill a few empty seats in the performing arts center because there would be big-name entertainment. So she called and said she would sell us two tickets for a small fraction of the four-figure price.

Tom and I bought the two tickets and figured we'd just use my flight attendant benefits and be gone from home only about twelve hours.

As we hopped on an almost-empty plane, I began

to wonder what other people at this party would be like. I had heard that one patron of the arts gave a one-time gift of eighty million dollars. I thought it might be interesting to attend a party where most of the 675 guests had more money than I could imagine. I wondered if they would be different, in looks or conversation, and if Tom and I could blend in and not be revealed for the aliens we were.

We arrived at the party and stepped into the courtyard of the outside reception. Immediately a stir surrounded us—like something you see on television with paparazzi.

My friend had apparently told all her friends who were on the staff at the arts center that Tom and I should be treated like the guests of honor. Which was a joke. I'm sure the price we paid for discounted tickets was the lowest donation of the evening.

But the stir at our entrance continued as we were introduced around. Someone mentioned we had just flown in from Savannah and had come straight from the airport. More people began to gather around us. The men asked my husband his line of business. My husband is a quiet, reserved man, so he said the name of his employer in one word and smiled. It just so happens that the name of my husband's employer is instantly recognizable by those who purchase private luxury jets.

Suddenly more guests were crowding around us. They said, "Did I hear you say your company is…?" and then look at Tom, as if they were talking to Santa Claus. Then they gushed enthusiastically, "We love your jets!"

Tom and I looked at each other in a moment of quiet, and I whispered to him, "Are these the customers for the fifty-million dollar jets you design?"

"It would appear so," he said, taking a sip of his sparkling water.

Soon more people came up to us, and some got personal: "What do you do for that company?" they asked Tom.

My husband is humble and honest. He looked them in the eye and said, "Engineer." And I, ever the supportive wife, said, "He's just being humble. He is so much more than just an aerospace engineer." And they laughed, as if we were all sharing a joke. "No, really," I said, confused by their laughter. "He is…" And I looked at Tom and said, "Tell them, honey." But Tom waved me away, because he doesn't like to draw attention to himself.

More and more people came up to us and wanted to talk about my husband's business. They wanted to tell us what they liked about every design of every luxury jet ever designed. Someone mentioned she had read that Jim Carrey bought one of the jets and paid only forty-four million.

And everyone, without fail, asked what I did, and I said, "I have two jobs really. I'm a part-time flight attendant and an author."

"Oh, really?" they said, and then they turned back to my husband and said, "We understand you flew out just for this party."

"Yes," Tom said, "and we have to go back tonight."

"So," they said, "you just flew out tonight, and then you're headed back to the airport to fly back tonight?"

I wanted these people to know it's a perk of my job, so I said, "It's nothing, really. I mean, we do fly free, you know."

Then the people laughed and elbowed Tom and said, "Perks of the job, huh?" Because we are used to that response, Tom answered the way he always does: "Yes! It's great!" (Tom has always loved that benefit of my job.)

And then they inquired about our jet ride out from Savannah to San Diego. And I told them, "Well, it was lovely. The plane was mostly empty, but it was great service, with dinner and a movie and a little nap, and we were here."

The people smiled knowingly. But somehow it seemed we weren't communicating on the same level—I couldn't put my finger on exactly how. Something was wrong. The people seemed way too impressed with the benefits of my job. Didn't they know any other flight attendants? I tried to tell a few people that we fly places for dinner a lot. In fact, I mentioned to several people that just the week before we flew to Rome for twenty-four hours.

After that, things got even stranger in the comment department. Someone came up and told me she loved my gown. I knew the gown was a version of another gown by a famous designer, and since I can't keep a good deal to myself, I told her, "I love it too. And you won't believe the deal I got on it. I bought it off the clearance rack for nineteen dollars." The people stared at me and then started laughing as if I'd made a joke. (My friends back home would have wanted the address of the clearance rack.)

By the end of the evening, when *San Diego Maga-*

zine said it wanted our names for the photo spread and asked me to twirl so the skirt of my dress flew out like in those pictures in the magazines of the rich and famous, I knew something was wrong.

"Tom," I said, "we did tell them that I'm a flight attendant/author and you are an engineer, right?"

"Yes."

"Well, do you think they think you own the company you work for or something?"

Before Tom could answer, someone came up to us and introduced herself as an executive for a world famous bank. She said quietly to my husband, "If you need anyone to finance your jet sales, I'm the one to talk to."

Tom politely took her card, looked her in the eye, and said sincerely, "Thank you."

And that's when we knew they didn't know who we were. They thought we were a couple who could borrow a fifty-million-dollar private jet to fly from one coast to another just to attend a party. They thought we were people so high up in the company my husband worked for that one of his perks was use of the company jet.

They had misconstrued all our conversations about free air travel and perks of the job and flying first class and these being no big deal. How did we explain to the entire group that we weren't who they thought we were?

We didn't. We couldn't. But weeks after we left the party, we realized that *San Diego Magazine* must have done some research, because my picture never did appear in that magazine. We were never listed as the "generous donors" they thought we were. And we never saw those people again.

We looked like them, but we sure weren't one of them.

Everybody's doing it.

*T*rust me, not everybody is doing it. But all
the ones who *are* doing it are very vocal about
it and want you to believe this lie is true.

Seeing is believing.

A new minister in town sent me an e-mail telling me he liked my writing and was wondering if my husband and I would like to visit his church sometime. From his comments about my writing, I knew he was a fine and intelligent chap. After visiting his church, I fear his congregation may not feel the same about me.

All was going well in the service. The music was good; the sermon was great. And then came the time for taking Communion. Now, I grew up in a church in which the Communion elements are passed and each person takes a bit of wafer and then a tiny cup of drink. But in this church people were invited to come forward and receive the elements from the hands of the church officers. The wafer was dipped in the cup and then put into each person's mouth.

Because I wasn't familiar with this and wasn't sure how it all worked, I decided I would stay seated for this service and just watch. My husband and daughter got up, and my husband urged me to follow them with a big motion of his hand. I shook my head no and sat still with my arms crossed. My husband got in line and urged me again with a larger hand motion while mouthing the words *Come on,* but I shook my head more vigorously no.

I'm sure the people behind us thought, *What kind of woman would split her family up during this holy partaking?* and scooted their children a little away from me. But whatever they thought was nothing compared to what they would be thinking just moments later.

I watched as Tom and Mandy walked up to get the wafer and then watched as it was dipped into the cup and put in their mouths. It wasn't until Tom received the wafer after Mandy that he turned to look at me with horror on his face, and I looked at him the same way. It suddenly occurred to both of us—at the exact same moment—that the wafer was a wheat cracker. Our daughter has celiac disease, which means her intestines blister if she eats any wheat, oats, barley, or rye. She absolutely cannot ingest gluten from any crackers, cakes, or pastries.

As Mandy was coming back to her seat, I jumped out of mine, put my hand under her mouth, and hissed urgently, "Spit it out! Spit it OUT! SPIT IT OUT!" And everyone around us saw the partially chewed remains of the body of Christ come out into my hand.

I'm sure the woman behind us who made the sign of the cross toward me thought the worst. I mean, what kind of mother interferes with her daughter's holy moment?

But you can't believe everything you see. I suppose that is why Jesus said, "Judge not." Only God has enough of the details of a person's life to judge her. We are told to love and pray for her. And after last Sunday, I probably have a whole church praying for me today.

Lies I Believed About Prayer

It's not a good idea
to pray for the same thing
over and over. You wouldn't
want to bug God.

~~

Actually, asking for the same thing over and over is a good way to get it. There is a story in the Bible about a judge and a woman who bugged him until he gave in to her request. *Nagging* is what the story sounded like to me. But Jesus said that asking over and over was good. God doesn't get mad about persistence in prayer—in fact, he encourages it.

Prayer doesn't
change anything.

∽

om once heard me pray a prayer that God
would open the windows of heaven and
rain down enough money to pay off our
bills. He said, "Prayers like that are not the answer to
credit card debt. And I don't think they will change a
thing."

What Tom means, of course, is that God wants
responsible behavior. But my answer back to Tom is, if
we can't come to God when we have been irrespon-
sible, then when can we come to him?

I mean, it was Jesus himself who said he came to
save the sick, not the well. (And I know he meant all
kinds of sick, including those who are sick from acting
irresponsibly.)

If prayer didn't change things, why would Jesus have bothered with it? Especially on the last night of his life, when he was sweating over what lay ahead and he felt so alone. Jesus clung to prayer in the last hours of his life because, although it didn't change the pain of the path God had given him to walk, it gave him strength, like food for the soul. Strength to go on. The path to joy is often filled with sorrow. And prayer gets us through.

If I don't deserve it,
I can't ask God for it.

❧

hen I hear people say this, I always want to ask those who believe this lie if they are parents. There is no way I would give my daughter only what she deserves. I adore her and will give her every possible good thing I can. That is how God feels about us. As a mother who gathers her children under her arms, as a father who has pity on his children, as a manager who wants people to run into his office with boldness—that is how God wants us to know him And that is how he relates to us. The whole idea of *grace* does away with the idea of our getting what we deserve.

I'll get used to it.

❧

I used to think that if God answered all my big prayers in life—like my prayers for a husband, a baby, a career—I wouldn't be surprised when he answered other prayers. I would get used to his goodness to me. But I don't get used to it. Every day it seems new.

God has answered so many of my prayers beyond my wildest dreams, and I'm still surprised with his generosity, daily. Maybe I'll never get used to it, not even in eternity.

Lies I Believed About Life

Life is supposed to be easy.

∾

Where did I get the idea that life is supposed to be easy? Sometimes I think it comes from the fairy tale about Cinderella. I mean, she had it hard in the beginning, but then it all came together for her—and I never did read that she had one problem as an adult.

I had lots of problems in the beginning of life, but somehow I thought problems would eventually stop. And they haven't. Take this last month. I was trying to finish a book that was due and no words were coming. So we had a writer with a book due and no words to put in it. This is stressful.

Then our old car broke down for the eighth time. We took it to the repair shop, but the repairman couldn't find a problem and gave it back to us. After the car broke down three times in the next twenty-four hours, we took it back to the repair shop and left it there for a week, where it ran perfectly, every day, never once even showing a hint of trouble. So the shop gave it back to us. And that's when we realized the car was taunting us. (I don't remember ever hearing in the story of Cinderella that the prince had transportation problems.)

Then my husband, who rarely goes to the doctor, began experiencing unexplained dizzy spells. That required lots of medical tests. And required me to take time off from writing.

One of Tom's tests came back indicating a symptom of cancer, so I took Tom to another doctor to have further tests done, which fortunately came back negative. Then our car broke down again—just stopped in the middle of the road.

The next week, Mandy's school called, and the nurse said she thought our daughter might have broken her leg because she wouldn't stand on it after a large kid had run into her and fallen across it. I drove to the school, headed straight for the nurse's office, and scooped up Mandy, who wouldn't put any weight on the leg. I carried Mandy to the car and drove her to the emergency room where I filled out all the paperwork and waited for what seemed like hours. We sat for two sets of x-rays and then the doctor came in and said Mandy's leg was fine, just a bad bruise. I looked at Mandy, as she jumped out of the wheelchair they had put her in and skipped out to the car.

Then the school called and said that even though the school bus has always picked my daughter up in front of her home, she would now have to walk across a busy intersection to be picked up. They also told me that if I didn't like it, I could take it all the way to the school board, which I didn't have time to do. (And which someone told me in advance probably wouldn't help.)

Then my husband came home and said that his work wasn't going well and where would I like to move if the layoffs hit? Then the scales in our bathroom broke. I mean, either they broke or I have gained five pounds in the last five days. And who could do that?

Things began to calm down just in time for a hurricane. Yes, a real hurricane. We live in a section of the United States that has a hurricane season, and this year Hurricane Isabel was headed straight for our home. And I thought that of all the excuses for me to give my editor about why I couldn't finish my new book, "There is a hurricane headed toward our house" was the most unbelievable. And yet true.

Life isn't easy. It wasn't easy in my childhood and it's not easy as an adult.

The thing I find interesting is that even people who have never read Cinderella or even heard of her have this same sense of what life "is supposed to be."

Where does this universal quest, this dream of perfection come from? I think it comes from a sense that we know there is perfection somewhere, if only we could find it.

"He has also set eternity in the hearts of men."

We'll catch up on sleep this weekend.

The first year of our dog's life, my husband and I worked very hard at training her not to bark at inappropriate times. We got the books and the videos and spoke to our sister-in-law who raises show dogs. We got the spray bottle with a bit of vinegar in the water and sprayed it in the dog's mouth when she would bark inappropriately. And it worked perfectly. Within just a few weeks, she was barking only if she was in distress or someone strange came into the yard.

Then came last Saturday morning. We were tired. Home on a rare Saturday when neither one of us had to get up early. We were looking forward to sleeping in.

At 6:14 A.M., our dog started making a fuss on the

deck near our bedroom door. So I kicked and pushed Tom out of bed, and he got her set up outside in her dog run.

At 7:10 A.M., we were back into a good sleep when Angel (yes, that's her real name) started barking her head off.

Waking from a sound sleep, I jumped out of bed saying words I don't want you to know. I ran outside in my old flannel pj's and noticed Angel had wrapped her chain around a tree and knocked over the large reserve water bottle, which was gurgling as all the water ran out. Angel is afraid of the water bottle anyway (because it gurgles loudly), and she looked terrified as it began sliding down the slope toward her. Her bark was warning it to stop where it was, to stop that sliding right now or face the consequences.

I untangled Angel, comforted her regarding the evils of an out-of-control water bottle, and then sneaked quietly back into the house, only to discover our daughter was now fully awake. And a short while later, so were the two girls who were spending the night.

If we lived in a perfect world, all dogs would have a program in their brains: "Don't bark when Master is sleeping unless Master is in danger." But we don't live in a perfect world now do we? And some intentions, like desperately attempting to sleep in on the only Saturday you get to sleep in, just don't go as planned.

If I have just had a checkup and everything is fine, I have nothing to worry about.

A fter a checkup at the doctor, the thing I worry about most is WMH. You may not have heard of WMH—but you've seen it in action. It is an acronym for What Might Happen. And mark my words, every person in America worries about it. In fact, people around the world have always known the horror of WMH. Since the first day the first mom sent the first son out without a coat on, people have worried about WMH.

And rightly so. I don't mean to alarm the Centers for Disease Control and Prevention here, but I have documentation proving that every person living today will contract some form of WMH. And die from it. Cease to live. Expire.

So we do have a lot to worry about. A great lot. The fatality rate of those with a strain of WMH is only one of the things we have to worry about. There is also the SHISICGIT disease, as in the "She Has It So I Could Get It Too" disease. Or the disease that is spread simply by saying the words, "You don't look well." I've rarely heard of someone who has been told those words who hasn't been sick shortly thereafter, unless, of course, she is a middle-aged woman—then it's just the normal fall of the face that makes her not look well.

So if the threat of WMH and SHISICGIT has been known since the beginning of time and was rampant even in the days of Rome, how is it that one Jew in Roman times was able to walk around saying, "Don't worry"? Over and over again, he said, "Don't worry. Don't worry. Don't worry."

Could it be that he didn't know about WMH? Or did he just trust his Creator?

Because I'll tell you one thing, if you don't have at least a little trust in your Creator, WMH could worry you sick.

Success does not come from failure.

❧

The movie *Seabiscuit* offers a minicourse in what it takes to succeed. In that movie, everyone gets a dose of bitterness, of hardship, of failure. Everyone is repeatedly knocked down and considered out. But then they get up and come back. And in the end, they all become winners—in at least one way.

I used to think that success was about winning. And not losing. But now I think it is about coming back from failure, not about never experiencing failure.

I've had so much failure in my life that if I were to get stuck in it, it would be like quicksand—quicksand with the weight of being embarrassed pulling me under the mire of stinging laughter from people who would never have been as stupid as I am.

But instead of wallowing in the quicksand of embarrassment for having tried something and failed, I want to be a person who realizes that getting up and starting over and pressing on after I have been knocked down is what success is.

Remind me of this the next time I fail, will you?

You can't legislate morality.

◦~◦

I always laugh when I hear a group that wants to legalize something that goes against some law of society say, "You can't legislate morality!"

Legislating morality is exactly what our judicial system is based on. Don't kill. Don't steal. Those laws are legislated morality. People in all countries have been legislating morality since the beginning of time—because people have realized since time began that if we let everyone run amuck and go their own way, they will go off the deep end. And I don't think I'm the first one to make that observation.

Going to the dentist
can't be fun.

❦

For years I hated going to the dentist, and then, in the decade before I wrote this book, I discovered the most wonderful dentist in the world. And even though my husband and I now live three thousand miles away, I still hop on a plane to go to all my dentist appointments. And I'm not the only one who travels thousands of miles just to visit this dentist. His office is in Edmonds, Washington, a town just north of Seattle, and he has patients who fly in from Alaska, California, and Georgia.

Is it because his office is fancy on the outside? No. Is it because he does massive advertising? No, he relies on word of mouth—pun intended.

Well, what is it exactly that makes Dr. Joe Albert so special?

Let me tell you what it is like to visit Dr. Albert's office.

First, you are stunned to find his office isn't carved in marble but is at the end of a small area of shops off a busy street. When you walk into the office, you are greeted by the smell of baking bread or fresh cookies. Immediately you love the place. (His assistants tell me they have found that people relax more when the place smells of things they love.)

Then—and I'm not kidding, this really happens— you are asked if you'd like to have a latte or a fresh brewed cup of coffee from a state-of-the-art machine that was brought in from Europe. (And let me tell you right now, you pay the same price at Dr. Albert's office as you do at any other good dentist's.) Then you are taken back to a room by your own "customer care" person, who gets you seated and takes your history. (I've never seen anyone wait for an appointment.) All the while you are sipping your coffee.

The chair you sit in is a standard chair for a patient, but you are handed a remote control for the full-length massage mat under you. You are given a minilesson in how to adjust the massage machine, so while you are waiting, your neck or back or legs are also loving this dentist and already begging you to come back. Then you are offered a headset pretuned to your preference in radio stations. Next, Dr. Albert comes to chat with you, and he is kind and humble. I think humility is the first thing you notice about him and then his kindness.

If you have a huge number of dental problems, as I've always had when I go to Dr. Albert, he sets out a treatment plan that fits your budget, and if it doesn't, he sets out a plan that fits your payments.

Now, Dr. Albert is not a religious man. He certainly doesn't believe in God as I do. But Dr. Albert is a living example of verses in the Bible about how putting others' needs before your own is a wonderful way to live. And, you know, it's a wonderful way to get loyal patients as well. It makes going to the dentist, well, downright fun.

The worst thing
about a full airplane
is screaming little kids.

❧

S creaming kids are not on *every* full airplane flight, but SAWs are. SAWs are the worst thing about a full flight, and they occur on every single full flight—without exception.

What is an SAW? It's a Seat Armrest War. SAWs are usually fought with looks and pokes and sighs and coughs, and only once in a while do they become violent. They are, nevertheless, horrible. I've been involved in many a low-level skirmish from an escalating SAW. Although I do have to say, after many years of observation, I've come to the conclusion that *men* are the biggest perpetrators of AHWIF—Armrest Hogging While in Flight. Resulting in SAWs.

Seat Armrest Wars. You know them. You've seen them. You've participated in them. Don't lie—unless you've never been in coach on a full flight, you've done it. You've looked down and seen that there aren't enough armrests in your row and those that are there won't accommodate even the arms of a child. I mean, on a standard, full, single-aisle plane, you've got four armrests at best and six arms. And if you're in the middle seat with people on either side of you, you don't stand a chance.

I've seen how it works. Seat A goes for the name-it-and-claim-it and spreads his elbows out, covering all the armrest for B. Then B arrives and tries to be polite to A and leans into C's space and covers all the C armrest. So what happens is poor C and B push and sweat and throw mean glances at each other—thus another SAW begins.

So what can be done about this common irritant? Well, I don't know. But one thing I do know: SAWs are an example of other situations in life. And how we respond to them says something about how we live in a world in which everybody seems to want what the other guy is trying to hog.

If God is pleased with me, I won't have hard times.

∽

A man named Jesus said he was God's son. And once, when Jesus was on earth, people saw a dove come down from heaven and go to Jesus, and a voice said, "This is my beloved Son, in whom I am well pleased." And it seemed to everyone who reported the story later that God was saying Jesus was very pleasing to him.

Yet, Jesus, as it is written, was mocked, spit on, beat down, and homeless, and he died in a place usually reserved for criminals, so I think that pretty much shoots down the lie that God won't allow hard times to come to those who please him.

Lies I Believed About Myself

I'm the only one who has ever done anything this dumb.

c~⁹

he world is full of people who have done things just as "not clearly thought through" as I have.

One of my favorite television shows is *World's Dumbest Criminals*. These are people who tried to pull off a crime without thinking the whole thing through. They act out of passion instead of self-control. Like the guy who decided to rob a store and put a paper bag over his head so he wouldn't be recognized but forgot to punch eyeholes in the bag. Or the security guard who decided to rob a store in a mall while on duty but forgot to take off his uniform, so even though he had a mask on, people knew who he was.

I can relate to these people. I would do something stupid like that if I ever got that far into crime. A Bible verse says that everybody in the whole world and throughout history has done something at some time that wasn't smart: "We all, like sheep, have gone astray, each of us has turned to his own way."

Are you the only one to do something as dumb as the last dumb thing you did? You're not. Others have gone before you, and others are beating you at being dumb at this very moment.

I just need to be patient.

everal years ago, when we moved into a small, old house, we were advised that the stains would never come out of the hardwood floors. So we installed carpet over the beautiful—but stained—hardwood floors.

Now, in the muddy northwest, or northwet as we referred to it, trying to keep carpet clean was impossible unless you were on constant dirt patrol. People naturally tracked in mud and rubbed it into the carpet. For years, I asked my husband to help me figure out what to do about the mud-stained carpet that ran the whole width of our little home. And for years, he said, "Yes, I will do that." And then it would get pushed down on my husband's priority list. Finally one day, I went nuts—more than usual—and got out the scissors and started hacking at the stains in the carpet. I cut down the middle of the carpet, cutting myself a line between one side of the house and the other. Then I folded back the carpet like the Red Sea to expose the hardwood floors underneath.

Tom came home as I was trimming off the excess carpet pieces. He looked at the parted carpet held back by the displaced furniture, hardwood floors running down the middle, and said calmly, "Did we have a little frustration today?"

That night, Tom mentioned that I had helped him "reorganize his priorities" and that suddenly "taking care of fixing the carpet" was at the top of his list. He went out and rented a floor sander and sanded down the hardwood floors where the carpet used to be. It only took a few hours. Then we had someone come in and apply wood stain for us. And it was all perfect.

Now, if I had chosen to sit and wait and wait, Tom—who tends to procrastinate—might still be saying, "I'll get to that."

Sometimes immediate action is what's required. That's all I want to say.

If I think about how bad it is for me, I'll avoid it.

❧

ou can tell me candy bars are bad for me all you want, but I'm still going to keep a whole bag of them in the refrigerator for a mental emergency. I know they are bad for me, but I keep them there because they cheer me up. I don't know why the media think telling us to act in a responsible way will make us act that way. People have been told since the beginning of time about things not to do, and do you think that's stopped us?

If I have five sets of keys to my car, I'll be able to find at least one set when I need it.

∼⌒∽

J am forever losing the keys to my car. (And may I make a social observation here? Have you noticed that in any given family, there is one person who loses the keys and one person who doesn't? What is the deal with that? But back to my specific problem.) I have five sets of keys to my one car, and I can never find one set. My husband has one set of keys to his one car, and he has never lost his keys. (I've never even seen him looking for them unless I have used them because I couldn't find mine and then lost them before I could return them to him.)

The deal is, and this is oh-so-embarrassing to admit, one time I lost one set, went into the house to get a spare, and was driving through town when someone flagged me down. When I opened my window to ask the person what she wanted, she pointed to the passenger door and said, "Keys. Your keys are hanging in the door lock." And so it was that I had left my keys in the passenger side door, forgotten they were there, and gone into the house to look for them. When I couldn't find them, I got another set and drove off, hearing a banging on the side of the door and thinking we really needed to get this car in for repair.

If God saves everything we have lost, there will be a mountain of keys awaiting me in heaven.

If I don't show talent for something, I should give it up.

❦

*I*f I had listened to some people who said, "You'll never make a living at writing" (when I had been working ten years at trying to write my first book), I would have been a fool.

Because even if you don't show talent for something at the beginning, hard work and continual practice can pave the way to success. If God has given you a dream, go for it. Work toward it. Be patient about it. And eventually it can happen, even if other people tell you it never will.

When God gave drive, he meant for us to use it to work toward our dreams. Even dreams someone else tells us are impossible.

When I meet a famous person, I will act in a calm and normal fashion.

❧

I've always thought that if I met someone famous, I would be clever and witty and calm and collected. Then I met two of my heroes: Anne Graham Lotz and Coach Pat Riley.

And, well, I wasn't who I thought I'd be.

First, Anne Graham Lotz. I've always admired Billy Graham's daughter, especially since I found out she is also an author and she also has a husband who has a tendency to see how far the car will go with its gas gauge near empty.

Now, I knew no one who knew anyone in the

Graham family, nor did I know anyone who knew anyone who knew anyone in the Graham family. And I didn't have a clue how to get in touch with Anne. I just had to pray about it. Then one day I decided to help God out, and I went online and found the number for Anne's organization and called there and tried to get someone to put Anne on the phone.

The people I talked to were very polite and treated me the same way you would treat an enthusiastic puppy: gentle and firm. And they didn't put me through to Anne's home, no matter how often I told them, "Anne would love me. I know she would."

So, after a couple more calls to them, over a period of a few weeks, I gave up and went back to praying God would arrange a meeting between Anne and me. It would have to be an answer to prayer, because my own efforts weren't working.

Then one day a few months later, I met her. I was in the terminal at Atlanta Hartsfield International, walking around waiting for my takeoff time, and I looked over and there sitting in a chair, reading a book, was this woman who looked exactly like Anne Graham Lotz. I walked up and stood right in front of her and stared down at her as if I were trying to figure out if she was human or a wax figurine. She looked up at me, and I think I was drooling on to her head, when I said, "You look like someone."

"I hope I am someone," she said, in a voice mixed with humor and gentleness.

I wiped my mouth with my sleeve. "Is your name Anne?" I said.

"Yes." And then she extended her hand, and as we shook hands, we said it together, only I said it with reverence. "Anne Graham Lotz."

"Oh my…" I said, and then I started babbling. "Hi, my name is Marsha Marks, and I think you'd really like this book I wrote. Oh yeah, I wrote a book, well actually two books. That's right, I am a genuine author. Well, I'm also a flight attendant. But I've only been doing that for eighteen years. And my husband is a lot like your husband, and I called your office, and I really wanted to meet you, my whole life, well, not my whole life, actually, it's only been in the last few years…" I could not shut up. But, it got worse.

I wanted to give Anne a book, but the only one I had with me had already been signed to my friends Chuck and Mary, so I started scratching out their names to put hers in, like a fool, and I just kept on babbling. Babbling about nothing, not even stopping to take a breath. In summary, let's just say that Anne and her husband were probably glad when my flight was called and I had to go. I don't need to tell you, this meeting didn't go as I planned.

Now, after hearing about my encounter with Anne, you probably think going mute in the presence of a celebrity would not be a problem for me. But as it turns out, I can be a fool of the mute kind as well.

The year was 1994, and my husband and I had been living in the Pacific Northwest for five years. Prior to that, we had lived for five years in Los Angeles.

Now, the entire time we lived in Los Angeles we were huge NBA Lakers fans. Actually, it was Tom who was the Lakers fan. I was a fan of Coach Pat Riley. I don't know what it was about Coach Riley, but I just adored the man. Maybe it was his height. I'm a tall woman, almost six feet in heels, and Coach Riley was six foot seven. Also, I am attracted to strong silent types. And Coach Riley was the epitome of the man who could accomplish a lot with a few words. I was also impressed by his ability to gather and motivate a group of enormous egos and undisciplined talent. And then there was the whole thing about his winning streak. Voted year after year as the overall best coach in the NBA. And don't even get me started on how nice this man looked in his perfect suits and ties. The truth was I felt Mr. Riley could just possibly be the most per-fect coach who ever lived.

So for years, I smiled just at the appearance of Coach Riley on television. During many a game, I prayed the coach would win, and God answered my prayers. But I never once prayed I could meet the coach. It seemed too far-fetched even for me to dream about. Then one night, I was on a layover in Portland, Oregon. It was about eight o'clock, and the streets were deserted. Our limo pulled up in front of the beautiful Benson Hotel, and the other two flight atten-dants got out and went into the hotel quickly. I lagged behind, getting my bags arranged and then wheeling them up the stairs to the front door of the hotel. I stopped on the second stair to adjust my coat, and when I looked down, I saw a pair of shoes in front of my bag. I heard a wonderful voice that seemed strangely familiar say, "Hello." And I let my eyes go up the pant leg from the shoe and up the coat sleeves and into the face of the voice. And then my mouth fell open and I went mute. Totally mute. I was staring into the face of Coach Pat Riley.

He stood there for a minute politely waiting for me to answer his greeting. I didn't. I just stared at him. Not even aware that my jaw was dropping more and more. I couldn't believe it. It was like he had stepped off television and into my life.

Coach Riley must have figured I was mute or something, because he turned and walked that cool walk up the remaining stairs and into the hotel. Once he was safely out of earshot, I started shouting, running up the other stairs with my bags dragging behind me and shouting to the bellmen on each side of the door. "Do you know who that was? Do you know who that was? That was Coach Riley. Pat Riley!"

"Yes," the bellmen said as they opened the door for me. "The Knicks are playing the Blazers tomorrow night."

Then I was in the lobby of the hotel, and there he was, the coach, not forty feet in front of me, standing at the lobby desk. I stumbled over my own feet trying to catch up to him.

"Mr. Riley," I said, sweating from running. "Mr. Riley, Mr. Riley." In his magnificent Iceman way, he turned and looked at me. He paused, and then with his classy coolness, he said, "Yes?"

And I, of course, stopped in my tracks and went mute again. He stood there, waiting for me to speak. And I stood there thinking, *My husband will never believe who I met tonight.* I was glorying in the moment, and Mr. Riley, I'm sure, just wanted to get out of the lobby.

Finally, just as he was turning to leave my silence, I found my voice. "Ahhhhhh," I said. "You are my favorite coach." And I wiped the sweat that was dripping off my forehead.

"Thank you," he said and smiled as he turned to go to his room.

My knees went weak. I looked around me and told anyone who would listen that *that* was Coach Pat Riley. Then I went to my room and called all the people I had ever known for the prior ten years and told them they were never going to believe who I had just met. No one did believe it. But it's the truth.

So I guess we don't always know how we will act in the presence of someone we admire. Sometimes we babble and sometimes we go mute. That's just the way it is.

It's all about me.

❧

*I*t all started in 1993 when we met this couple at our church in Seattle. Their names were Chuck and Mary Kingsford-Smith. We hadn't known them very long when someone came up to us and asked us if we knew "who" the Kingsford-Smiths were.

"Of course we do," we said. "They are great people. Chuck is an engineer, and Mary is the greatest dinner hostess in the world."

"No," insisted our informer. "Do you know who they are? Who Chuck's father was?"

When we shook our heads no, we were told that the late Sir Charles Edward Kingsford-Smith was the "Charles Lindbergh of Australia," and his son Chuck Kingsford-Smith was our new friend. And that the Sydney airport is named the Kingsford Smith International Airport.

Well, we were dutifully impressed—more at the humility of our new friends in not announcing "who they were" than at the discovery of their famous parent.

Over the next few years, we saw Chuck and Mary several times a week, and they became very close friends. And several times we met with Chuck's mother, the former Lady Kingsford-Smith, the widow of the aviator famous for making the first flight across the Pacific.

In fact, it was on a day when the former Lady Kingsford-Smith was visiting Seattle that Tom called me from his job at Boeing Commercial aircraft company. He was very excited and a little out of breath from running to the phone to tell me some news he seemed stunned to report.

"Marsha," he said, almost yelling, "they have just rolled out the new triple 7 for British Airways. And British Airways names all its jets. You are *never* going to believe whose name is on the side of the first jet."

Well, I knew a few people thought I was going to be famous as a writer someday, but so far, I'd only had a few articles and short stories published. So I was as shocked as Tom was. "You're kidding!" I said. "I can't believe it! They named the jet Marsha? Marsha!"

"No," said Tom. And his voice took on the dryness

it gets when he realizes anew how his wife's brain actually works. "They named the jet Sir Charles Edward Kingsford-Smith." After Chuck's father.

I was thrilled for Chuck and Mary but sorely crushed to realize that what I'd thought was going to be early recognition for writing-yet-to-be-discovered was, in fact, not about me at all.

Acknowledgments

ere are the people who really should have been thanked before now:

Connie Smiley, who is without fail ever-ready to hear my writing in its rough stages and who is gentle and honest and loving—which I think are the attributes of a saint.

Sue Farren, who was finishing her first book while I was finishing this manuscript and who understands my phobias...and loves me in spite of them.

My editor, Elisa Fryling Stanford, whose face should be in *Webster's* under the word *great*.

My publisher, Don Pape, who is more than a publisher; he has an ear for talent, an eye for the suffering artist, and a heart for what is good and right. What more could you ask of a publisher?

And of course, my husband, Tom, and my daughter, Mandy Joy, who allow me to pursue my dream and who pray for me all along the way.

I have this great desire to write a long list of really

famous celebrity names here, thinking that if I thanked them personally for their contributions to this book, you'd believe I knew them, and how cool would that be?—except of course, it would be a lie.

So I'll end this by saying that every person I come in contact with in some way contributes to what I write, and that's the truth.

About the Author

*M*arsha Marks is a popular speaker and author known for her ability to blend humor with spiritual insights. She is the author of *101 Amazing Things About God, 101 Simple Lessons for Life,* and a former contributing editor to *Campus Life.* Her articles and stories have appeared in such publications as *Writer's Digest, Eternity, Moody Monthly,* and *The Christian Reader,* and she has appeared on numerous radio and television programs, including the Billy Graham Evangelistic Association's *Hour of Decision.* Her column, "A Few Minutes with Marsha," appears weekly in the *Effingham Herald.* Marsha and her family make their home in Savannah, Georgia.

Please visit Marsha at www.marshamarks.com or write to her at marsha@marshamarks.com.

A portion of the author proceeds from this book will be donated to www.supportawriter.com.

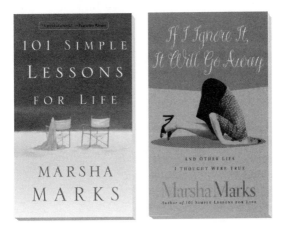

To learn more about WaterBrook Press and view our catalog of products, log on to our Web site:

www.waterbrookpress.com

WATERBROOK
PRESS